LOST LESSONS 2
A devotional by teens for teens

By
Dr. Randy T. Johnson
and
David Rutledge

© 2011 Randy Johnson

Published by:
Rochester Media, Inc
PO Box 80002
Rochester, MI 48308
248-429-READ (7323)
248-430-8799 fax
info@rochestermedia.com
www.rochestermedia.com

    All rights reserved. No part of this book may be reproduced or transmitted in any form or by any means including, but not limited to, electronic or mechanical, photocopying, recording, or by any information storage and retrieval system without written permission from the publisher, except for the inclusion of brief quotations in review.
    All Scripture quotations, unless otherwise indicated, are taken from Holy Bible, New International Version NIV ® copyright © 1973, 1978, 1984 by International Bible Society.

    Take note that the name satan and associated names are not capitalized. We choose not to give him any preeminence, even to the point of violating grammatical rules.

Author: Dr. Randy T. Johnson, David Rutledge
Cover Design: Brian Jamieson

First U.S. Edition Year 1st Edition was Published

Publisher's Cataloging-In-Publication Data

Johnson, Randy and Rutledge, David

Lost Lessons 2
Summary: Christian devotional based on the television series Lost (r).

13 Digit ISBN 9781461047469

1.Christian Living, Spiritual Growth, Lost, Christianity, Religion

For current information about releases by Dr. Randy T. Johnson or David Rutledge or other releases from Rochester Media, Inc., visit our web site: http://www.rochestermedia.com

Printed in the United States of America

Preface

LOST Lessons was written by Randy Johnson and David Rutledge. The book is well received and is reaching varied individuals. Young adults who are dedicated followers of Jesus Christ are learning to see media, Hollywood and even the world from a Christian perspective, while those who aren't necessarily connecting with a church are seeing Jesus in a fresh way. Based on this success, the authors decided to write on Season 2 of LOST, but with a twist: they involved 27 high school juniors and seniors:

Cullen Burgess	Naomi Issac
Zachary Preuss	Spencer Cameron
Trevor Katona	AustinPuckett
Erica Cosby	Branden Kowalyszyn
Justin Reckker	Adam Exelby
Kelsey Lucas	Annie Smither
Ariel Harris	Jack Lucido
Caleb Stanko	Ryan Hatfield
Audreanna Marazita	Patrick Vanbiesbrouck
Parker Higgins	Peter Mason
David Watts	Spencer Hodges
Timothy Pontzer	DaLindra Williamson
Max Howard	Joshua Prantera
Alexander Zito	

LOST Lessons 2 is designed as a "devotional by teens, for teens." This class of 27 students at Oakland

Christian School broke into small groups, watched an episode of LOST, discussed the spiritual implications and then wrote a devotional. Randy Johnson and David Rutledge gave direction and modified the lessons, striving to ensure good Biblical support and a flow that is easier to read. Each lesson begins with a pretty extensive overview of the episode, so someone who hasn't watched the show can still benefit from the devotional.

Randy Johnson and David Rutledge would like to say a special thank you to Tom Gendich and Rochester Media for believing in youth and publishing LOST Lessons 2 and a thank you to the other professionals who helped:

Laura Hall (http://rebornagain2010.wordpress.com/about-me/) edited the lessons for clarity, spelling and grammar.

Dr. Joe Cilluffo (web.me.com/jcilluffo) is the photographer.

Brian Jamieson (http://www.wix.com/jamiesondesign/Jamieson Design) designed the cover and the book layout.

A devotional by teens for teens

By
Dr. Randy T. Johnson
and
David Rutledge

Table of Contents

1. Diversifying Your Faith — 1
2. Are You Him? — 7
3. Having Faith When In Doubt — 13
4. Responsibility Is NOT Easy As Pie — 21
5. Filling That Empty Space — 27
6. Faith In The Physical — 35
7. The Tail End Of The Story — 41
8. The Silent Victory — 49
9. Lost And Forgotten — 57
10. Confession Time — 63
11. Who Is More Important? — 71
12. God's Healing Water — 77
13. Deceit From The Devil — 85
14. The Whole Truth, And Nothing But — 91

15.	The Greatest Sacrifice	99
16.	Fixing Our Mistakes	105
17.	Light Of The World	111
18.	To Eat, Or Not To Eat	117
19.	Be Still	132
20.	Courage Against Revenge	131
21.	What Is God's Plan?	139
22.	A Monumental Sacrifice	147
23/24.	What pushes your button?	153
About the Authors		161

Diversifying Your Faith

Episode 1
"Man of Science, Man of Faith"

The hatch is open. Locke is anxious to go inside, but Jack refuses to let the people down, as it seems very dangerous. In a series of flashbacks, Jack's approach on life is seen. In a "lifeboat" scenario, he chooses to help Sarah over another dying patient. After surviving the emergency ordeal, Sarah is told she has a broken back and nothing can be done. This leads to a debate between Jack and his father on bedside manner versus false hope. Jack goes for a run, tour de stade, and meets Desmond. Desmond asks why Jack is so frustrated. He describes the helplessness of Sarah's case and mocks the thought of a miracle. Desmond is surprised as he states more than asks, "You don't believe in miracles." The pinnacle flashback has Jack apologizing to Sarah as she sees her toes wiggle. Finally, when Jack, Locke and Kate are captured by Desmond, Jack takes a shot at Locke's faith by saying, "Is this your destiny?"

Locke is the man of faith. He is loyal to an unknown Island. He talks about sacrifice and destiny. The apostle Peter showed great faith when he stepped out on the water to go to Jesus (Matthew 14:22-29). Peter showed blind faith when he took that first step off the boat, having no idea what would happen. It was very possible that he could drown in the raging waters. All the other disciples just watched in wonder. Peter showed blind faith, and John Locke shows similar faith when he tries again and again to open the hatch, and when he descends into it.

Genesis 22 is a beautiful picture of faith. Abraham sets off to sacrifice his son of the promised generation. Hebrews 11:17-19 reveals his thoughts:

> By faith Abraham, when God tested him, offered Isaac as a sacrifice. He who had embraced the promises was about to sacrifice his one and only son, even though God had said to him, 'It is through Isaac that your offspring will be reckoned.' Abraham reasoned that God could even raise the dead, and so in a manner of speaking he did receive Isaac back from death.

Abraham took God at His word; he stepped out in major faith. Thomas Aquinas said, "Faith has to do with things that are not seen and hope with things that are not at hand." Faith isn't necessarily easy, just right.

Jack is the realist, a man of science. He is

skeptical and needs proof. The life of Thomas sounds similar. Thomas didn't believe Jesus had risen from the dead, and wouldn't believe it until he saw and felt the wounds on his hands and his side (John 20:25-29). A week later, Jesus appears to the twelve disciples and Thomas believes when he feels the nail marks in his hands and the mark on his side. In verse twenty-nine, Jesus says, "Blessed are those who have not seen and yet have believed." Jack, very much like Thomas, does not have blind faith. He believes when he sees, as he believed when he saw Sarah's miracle firsthand.

Exodus 3 records the call of Moses. Although he is known as a man of faith and total Moses needed proof. God gave him several samples of His power: his hand withering and being restored, water to blood, and his staff turning into a snake. After talking with God face to face, he still requested that Aaron can go with him. Victor Hugo said, "A faith is a necessity to a man. Woe to him who believes in nothing." Faith is crucial.

As Christians, we have to take some things blindly. There are just some things we have to take by faith. But we can't take everything blindly. The Bible tells us to defend our faith, not only for the sake of bringing others to faith, but also to deepen our relationship with Christ. 2 Timothy 2:15 says, "Do your best to present yourself to

God as one approved, a worker who does not need to be ashamed and who correctly handles the word of truth." Students are encouraged to study math, science, history and especially the Bible. 2 Timothy 3:16 reminds believers, "All Scripture is God-breathed and is useful for teaching, rebuking, correcting and training in righteousness." Believers need to continue to study Scripture to know how to grow in Christ as they are trained in right living.

Who do you relate to more: Locke or Jack?

_____

What are some things we have to take by blind faith?

_____

_____

_____

_____

_____

What are some ways to improve our abilities to defend our faith?

_____

Diversifying Your Faith

_____

_____

_____

_____

_____

Faith consists in believing when it is beyond the power of reason to believe –Voltaire

Are You Him?

Episode 2
"ADRIFT"

At the end of season one, Michael, Sawyer, and Jin are on a raft attempting to get off the island, but they are attacked by a mysterious boat. Sawyer is shot, and Walt is taken by the men on the ship. In Episode two of season two, we pick up this story as we see Sawyer and Michael arguing and struggling to get back to the island on a destroyed raft. Once they arrive on shore, they see Jin running out of the woods, his hands tied behind his back, screaming "Others." The three of them are captured and thrown into a pit. During all this, we see flashbacks of Michael struggling to keep custody of his son Walt. Michael eventually gives up custody, and we see Michael give Walt a toy polar bear as they say good bye in the park.

Meanwhile at the hatch, after Kate disappears into the hatch, John lowers himself down only to find Kate unconscious in the computer room. Desmond walks up behind John with a gun and asks him a very strange question: "Are you him?" John answers yes, but cannot answer the riddle to confirm the identity. Desmond ties Kate up and locks her in a dark room, but not before John slips her a knife. After locking Kate in the dark room, Desmond hears the beeping noise that signifies that it's the time to enter the code "4-8-15-16-23-42" and forces John to do it. The episode ends with Jack and Desmond meeting again.

When Desmond and John meet, Desmond asks John an interesting question. With a hopeful look, he asked, "Are you him?" John claimed to be, but was quickly proven an imposter. The question Desmond asked John is the same question that the Jews asked Jesus when He came to this earth, "Are you Him?" Are you the Messiah we have been waiting for, the Savior promised to us in the Old Testament prophecies?

The Jews were eagerly awaiting this person, this Messiah. They had prophecies of a Messiah sent from God to deliver them. They had prophecies about where he would come from, how he would die, and even what would happen to his clothing after he was killed. While Jesus was here on earth, people were asking, "Are you Him?" Mark 14:61-62 records that Jesus did claim to be the Messiah of the Old Testament. Mark 14 says, "Again the high priest asked him, 'Are you the Messiah, the Son of the Blessed One?' 'I am,' said Jesus..." So Jesus was claiming to be the expected Messiah. He was claiming to be the person that these people had been waiting for. He claimed to fulfill every prophecy written and be their everlasting hope.

But it's not enough to just claim to be the Messiah - you have to prove it. At every turn in Jesus life, He proved to be the Messiah. There are over 300 prophecies written about the coming Messiah in the Old Testament and Jesus fulfilled everyone. Some of these were written hundreds of years before Jesus was born, yet he still fulfilled them. It was prophesied that the Messiah was to be born in Bethlehem (Micah 5:2) and to be born of a virgin (Isaiah 7:14). It was prophesied that the Messiah would be betrayed by one of his own followers (Psalm 41:9) and killed by crucifixion (Psalm 22:14,16,17). And after His death, people would to cast lots for his clothes (Psalm 22:18).

Jesus fulfilled all of these prophesies and every other one written in the Old Testament. Even ones that happened that were out of His control. The difference between John Locke and Jesus is that Jesus was who He said he was. Jesus IS what we have been waiting for in our lives if we don't know him already. Jesus IS our hope and everything else he claims to be.

Would you have trusted Jesus if he told you he was the Messiah?

_____

_____

_____

_____

How would you put your trust in Him now?

_____

_____

_____

"Are you Him?" is a question we all have to ask ourselves. Who do you believe that Jesus is? Who do you believe that Jesus was?

_____

_____

_____

Are You Him?

I am trying here to prevent anyone saying the really foolish thing that people often say about Him: "I'm ready to accept Jesus as a great moral teacher, but I don't accept His claim to be God." That is the one thing we must not say. A man who was merely a man and said the sort of things Jesus said would not be a great moral teacher. He would either be a lunatic -on a level with the man who says he is a poached egg- or else he would be the Devil of Hell. You must make your choice. Either this man was, and is, the Son of God: or else a madman or something worse. You can shut Him up for a fool, you can spit at Him and kill Him as a demon; or you can fall at His feet and call Him Lord and God... –C.S. Lewis

Having Faith When In Doubt

Episode 3
"Orientation"

Locke is the featured character. His flashbacks start with his "last" support group meeting. It is here where he meets Helen. They start spending a lot of time together, and she realizes that he regularly slips out just to sit in his car outside his con-artist father's estate. Helen gives Locke a key to her place, but attaches the mandate that he get over his father issues. He breaks the agreement, so she shows up at the house, bumps into his car, throws his keys over the fence and challenges him to choose between her and his father. He says he doesn't know how. She responds for him to take a "leap of faith."

Meanwhile, Michael, Sawyer and Jin are captured and meet Ana Lucia. As the computer is shot and the orientation film is watched, new topics arise: Dharma Initiative, electromagnetic station, 108 minutes, and "Just saving the world." Within all the tension, Jack asks Desmond if he ever wondered if pushing the button was just a mind game. "Every single day," is Desmond's quick response. Jack is bewildered by the fact that Desmond has lived in a hatch and lived by a code where he pressed a button every 108 minutes on faith alone. The end of the episode brings Locke and Jack back together. Locke asks Jack, "Why do you find it so hard to believe?" Jack gives the logical quip back, "Why do you find it so easy?" In a stunning close, Locke says, "It's never been easy. It's a leap of faith."

This episode sounds easy to "spiritualize." It talks about "saving the world" and a "leap of faith." However, doubt is a topic often ignored. One feels guilty to ever admit it. Frederick Buechner said, "Whether your faith is that there is a God or that there is not a God, if you don't have any doubts, you are either kidding yourself or asleep. Doubts are the ants in the pants of faith. They keep it awake and moving." One shouldn't ignore doubt nor should one rest in it. Recognize it and research it. Find the truth.

Thomas is the most common Biblical character associated with doubt, but since he was referenced in the first devotion and since there are other godly individuals that can direct us, Gideon is chosen. The angel of the LORD comes to Gideon in Judges 6 saying, "The LORD is with you, mighty warrior" (verse 12). Gideon is called a mighty warrior. He is reminded that the LORD is with him and yet his response in verse 15 drips of doubt, "Pardon me, my lord," Gideon replied, "but how can I save Israel? My clan is the weakest in Manasseh, and I am the least in my family." History records on how Gideon's army was downsized from 32,000 to 10,000 to 300. His army being reduced to 300 soldiers against 125,000 Midianites was not the obvious cure for doubt. But, then God stepped in. Romans 8:31 reminds and encourages, "What, then, shall we say in response to these things? If God is for us, who can be against us?"

Doubt comes in all shapes and sizes. Sometimes doubt lasts but for a moment when we entertain an idea contrary to our current faith. Other times doubt lasts for a significant period of our lives, either constant or recurring for years, or even a lifetime. Some people doubt particular aspects or specific doctrines of our faith-- such as the Virgin Birth (Matthew 1:23) or the parting of the Red Sea (Exodus 14:21) or some of the miracles in the Gospels. Other people wrestle with things that are at the heart of our faith, such as the Trinity or the identity of Jesus -- who is Jesus of Nazareth? Is He Teacher and Prophet, or Messiah and Savior? Some people, like Thomas, have difficulty believing in the bodily resurrection of Christ. And still others wonder if there is a God at all.

That's the human experience when it comes to

God. We can't see God. It is hard for us to mentally comprehend the reality of the unseen. We can't touch God physically, or hear His voice audibly. We can only see His gifts to us: creation, human love, forgiveness, beauty, creativity, and Scripture.

God's greatest gift to us is Jesus Christ. Focus on Him, study Him, and believe you will discover God. Philip Yancey writes, "When in doubt, I focus on Jesus, the most unfiltered revelation of God's own self." Thomas believed when he saw the Risen Christ. He was captivated by him and instantly pledged his life and obedience to Him: "My Lord and my God!"

Faith is not something which can be scientifically rationalized, because rationalizing can be somewhat disappointing in its conclusions. Thomas thought that he needed concrete evidence, and failed to realize that he ignored the abstract, and the very core that makes up faith.

Why is it understandable for you to have doubt? First of all, remember that doubt is normal. Everyone has it from time to time. Yet, make sure you ask yourself where the doubt is coming from. Some people say that doubt comes from Satan. Maybe it does, but that simplifies the doubt to a point where it is easy to just let it fester. Get into the dirty of why you are questioning your faith. Is it because something bad happened? Is it because someone else of a different faith believes so strongly, and you don't think you are as passionate? Is it because God just seems so far away? Truly examine why you doubt so you can face these questions head on.

So, once you understand why you doubt your faith, you can begin to do something about it. The easiest way to deal with it is to pray about it. Spend some time alone with God talking it out. Let Him know what you are facing and ask Him to strengthen your faith. Even if it is hard to believe He is listening, because sometimes He feels so far away when we have doubts. But realize that He is always there.

What doubts do I have about my own ability?

_____

_____

_____

_____

If I overcame these doubts, how could God use me in a special way?

_____

_____

_____

_____

"What doubts do I have concerning faith?

_____

_____

_____

_____

Who should I talk to about getting answers?

_____

_____

_____

_____

"There can be no hope when there lacks interest for better. There can be no trust when there lacks confirmation of truth. There can be no faith when there lacks complete confidence of purpose."

– Adlin Sinclair.

Responsibility is NOT easy as pie

Episode 4
"Everybody Hates Hugo"

Hurley is dealing with food. As the biggest guy on the Island, this is an understandable thing. In this episode, we find Hurley struggling with his role on the Island. He is put in charge of taking inventory of and dispersing the food that was found in the hatch, but the task brings back some bad memories. During the flashbacks we learn that when Hurley won the lottery, everything and everybody changed. People did not like him as much, and he lost a lot of good things in his life. He does not want that to happen again.

Meanwhile, as Jack and Sayid inspect the hatch, Sawyer and Michael learn that their captors are survivors from the tail section of Oceanic 815. They are taken to a DHARMA initiative station where they meet the few remaining survivors of the tail section. They learn of the very difficult times the tail section has been through.

As the episode continues to focus on Hurley, we see him so worried over his situation that he thinks of blowing up the food to get rid of the problem, but is talked out of it by Rose. Still distraught, Hurley confronts Locke with the problem. He says that he does not want to do his job anymore. Locke says, "I had a lot of jobs that I didn't want to do. I still did them." He is pointing out that people should be satisfied with the jobs that they do, that they are given them for a reason, and that they should buckle down and get them done.

Salvation for a Christian is not the end - it's just the beginning. When we believe in God and accept His gift of forgiveness, we get the privilege of stepping into God's story. We get to be a part of the battle that has been going on since the fall; the battle between good and evil, the battle between God and the devil, playing out for the control of the world. God calls us to join His kingdom, to fight for him. God chooses to use us in the battle, and we are expected to find our role.

We each have a job to do as part of God's kingdom. We are each part of the body tasked by God to do our part. The jobs may be hard at times, they may seem like no-win situations, and we may be jealous of others jobs. But each person's task is given by God. It is our responsibility to do it to the best of our ability and be thankful for that we are given the opportunity to step into God's plan. Paul writes to the church in Corinth that everybody in the church has a specific job and that we should do the jobs that we are assigned:

> If the whole body were an eye, where would the sense of hearing be? If the whole body were an ear, where would the sense of smell be? But in fact God has placed the parts in the body, every one of them, just as he wanted them to be. If they were all one part, where would the body be? (1 Corinthians 12: 16-19).

In the same vein, in Genesis, Joseph had to struggle through some very hard times while attempting to follow God. He was sold into slavery by his brothers and even thrown into jail for living out his faith. In the midst of all this, Joseph was still faithful. When the time came for Joseph, he was ready. He used his gifts and ability to fight for God's kingdom, and God used him to save his family and entire countries from a terrible famine. As Christians, we need to step into the task that God has given us. It may not always be easy, it may not always be fun, but we know that we are serving the one true God. If we cultivate and nurture our gifts, God will be able to use us for magnificent things.

How should we respond to our gifts?

_____

_____

_____

_____

Are you thankful? Are you using your gift?

_____

_____

_____

_____

Could God have given us our gifts for a purpose? How do we fit into that purpose?

_____

_____

_____

_____

Responsibility is NOT easy as pie

"A winner is someone who recognizes his God-given talents, works his tail off to develop them into skills, and uses these skills to accomplish his goals." –Larry Bird.

Filling That Empty Space

Episode 5
"...And Found"

This episode focuses on losing something. Sun loses her wedding ring, Michael loses his son, Jin loses his friend and his job, and Mr. Eko loses the cap to his water bottle. While Jin and Mr. Eko search for Michael, Sun searches for her ring, which musters up some flashbacks. She remembers having an arranged date with a Harvard man, only to find out he had already found the one he loved. Her search for her wedding ring takes her from washing clothes with Claire, to Hurley accusing the dog, to Locke who says he isn't lost anymore because he stopped looking to Jack, saying that when he lost his ring he just made a replica. Finally, she and Kate dig up the buried bottle and find Sun's ring in the sand.

Fortunately, the joy right after losing something is finding something. It is the mystery of lost and found. After Jin loses his job, he walks by the waterway where he sees a woman wearing an orange dress. He remembers hearing that the family heirloom says his color for finding love today was orange. Just then he literally runs into Sun. Their eyes connect.

Every person is born feeling as if they have a hole in their heart. As Jack says," It's crazy where you will look when you want to find something bad enough." We can see this in the story of Zacchaeus, a Jewish tax collector. Once he meets Jesus, he gives up half of everything he owns to the poor and pays back everyone he stole from, in service to Jesus. He sees that only Jesus can make him content from within. Luke 19:1-10:

Jesus entered Jericho and was passing through. A man was there by the name of Zacchaeus; he was a chief tax collector and was wealthy. He wanted to see who Jesus was, but because he was short he could not see over the crowd. So he ran ahead and climbed a sycamore-fig tree to see him, since Jesus was coming that way. When Jesus reached the spot, he looked up and said to him, 'Zacchaeus, come down immediately. I must stay at your house today.' So he came down at once and welcomed him gladly. All the people saw this and began to mutter, 'He has gone to be the guest of a sinner.' But Zacchaeus stood up and said to the Lord, 'Look, Lord! Here and now I give half of my possessions to the poor, and if I have cheated anybody out of anything, I will pay back four times the amount.' Jesus said to him, 'Today salvation has come to this house, because this man, too, is a son of Abraham. For the Son of Man came to seek and to save the lost.'

It appears that Zacchaeus had tried to fill the void in his life with money. Once he found completion in Jesus Christ, he no longer was ruled by his money. He then was free to give and was compelled to right any of his wrongs.

People look to fill that hole with anything they can find. This could mean turning to money, cars, sex, or anything else that might fulfill their earthly desires. God tells us to look to Him. He tells us that He is the only one who can make us completely content. Looking for treasures on earth will not transcend into eternal peace - this is stated in Mathew 6:20-21: "But store up for yourselves treasures in heaven, where moths and vermin do not destroy, and where thieves do not break in and steal. For where your treasure is, there your heart will be also."

A person's ability to try and find contentment is not a right to turn his back on God. Choice in the matter is a gift from God - it does not mean that He is not the answer to the question, but rather that He wants us to find the answer on our own. He wishes for us to choose Him before the earthly desires. If those desires were not part of the choice, we would not need to choose Him; our decision would have already been made. As Solomon writes in the book of Ecclesiastes, about the struggles of filling his empty space, he describes what he turned to in order to feel complete. At the end of the book, he comes to a final conclusion on the matter. His conclusion is as follows in Ecclesiastes 12:13-14: "Now all has been heard; here is the conclusion of the matter: Fear God and keep his commandments, for this is the duty of all mankind. For God will bring every deed into judgment, including every hidden thing, whether it is good or evil." Fortunately, Solomon did not just stop looking as Locke stated. He wasn't content until he examined everything. When all was said and done, he found that only God could fill the gap and bring purpose to life.

What do you daydream about?

_____

_____

Filling That Empty Space

_____

_____

_____

What are the 3 things you think about the most?

_____

_____

_____

_____

_____

What are your priorities in life?

_____

_____

_____

_____

_____

Make a list of your top 8 priorities, where does God fit in?

_____

_____

_____

_____

_____

_____

_____

_____

_____

_____

_____

_____

_____

_____

_____

_____

Filling That Empty Space

"Illusion is needed to disguise the emptiness within."
–Arthur Erickson

Faith in the Physical

Episode 6
"Abandoned"

In this episode, as Ana-Lucia and the survivors of the back half of the plane travel with Sawyer, Michael and Jin toward Jack's camp, we see Sayid and Shannon move their relationship forward with a romantic date on the beach; however, their day is interrupted when Shannon suddenly sees Walt near the edge of the woods. She tries to explain this to Sayid, but he thinks it is a delusion. When Sayid does not believe her, Shannon takes off with Vincent looking for Walt.

During the flashbacks, we learn that Shannon has had to deal with the people in her life abandoning her. We also learn of her father's sudden death, how she was cut off from her inheritance and how even Boone leaves her to work for their step-mother. Back in the present, we see Shannon fearful of being abandoned again. After running off to the woods and finding Boone's grave, she decides once again to search for Walt. Sayid, after searching for Shannon for quite some time, finally finds her and tries to convince her to give up the search. But Shannon will not; she is mad at Sayid for not believing her, and she is afraid he will abandon her. After Sayid hears this, he reconciles with her and the pair embraces. In the next moment, they both hear whispers and look up to see Walt again standing off in the distance. They both run to him, but Sayid trips and while on the ground, hears a gunshot from ahead. Sayid then runs ahead in time to catch a falling Shannon. The episode then ends with Ana-Lucia holding the smoking gun.

In our lives, just as Shannon's, we can fear abandonment. Many can relate to Shannon's situation where her relationships are flawed and broken, and she is in a state of continual fear of abandonment. This fear consumes Shannon's mind until she can no longer have normal loving relationships and lives only to pursue immoral spirits of self-satisfaction and slothful indulgence. For Christians, we do not need to fear God abandoning us. Psalm 34:18 says, "The LORD is close to the brokenhearted and saves those who are crushed in spirit."

Joseph's life is a great example of this. In Genesis 37:12-28, Joseph, who was the most favored of his father, was tending his flock one day when his brothers conspired against him. Joseph's brothers lured him away from the home and stripped him of his multicolored robe and sold him into slavery. For Joseph, feeling abandoned would have been only natural after undergoing this kind of cruelty. Nothing else could have been expected from him. But the thing is, he did not feel this way. Instead of placing his security and happiness in physical things and human relationships, Joseph had his faith in God. Joseph understood that God always has a plan for his people and that he could never possibly expect to fully understand what it is. Joseph understood Psalm 16:8 (NIV), when it says; "I keep my eyes always on the LORD. With him at my right hand, I will not be shaken." Because of this, not only did he find peace in God, but he was also able to forgive and rectify his relationships with his brothers.

Oddly enough, no matter how much this message is preached, people still tend to forget. God will never abandon us. God not only loves the whole world, but he loves the individual too. Psalm 37:28 says: "For the LORD loves the just and will not forsake his faithful ones." God does not care about how intelligent, strong, or beautiful a person is; instead He cares about a person's love for Him. Psalm 27:10 (NLT) reminds us that "Even if my father and mother abandon me, the Lord will hold me close." God is love, and he is only waiting for you to come to him.

In what ways have you felt abandoned, and how do you restore balance?

_____

_____

_____

_____

Are you relying on human relationships over your relationship with God?

_____

_____

_____

_____

Why is it so important to make God your ultimate comforter, and how can you make him your ultimate comforter?

_____

_____

Faith in the Physical

_____

_____

_____

"God loves each one of us as if there were only one of us." –St. Augustine

The Tail End of the Story

Episode 7
"The Other 48 Days"

"The Other 48 Days" is different from previous episodes, because it follows the story of the survivors of the tail section of the plane. It starts with the tail section and debris falling into the ocean a short distance from shore. There are few survivors. The remaining survivors make camp on the shore. The second night, three of them are abducted, and Eko kills two of the attackers and then doesn't speak for forty days after that. Another man named Nathan encourages the group to stay on the beach despite the protest of Ana Lucia. After ten more days of struggle, nine more members are taken away by the "Others." They all go into the jungle being led by Ana Lucia. Ana makes camp and digs a pit, throwing Nathan into it, believing he is to blame. Nathan is freed by Goodwin, who then kills him anyway. On the 24th day, the survivors find a DHARMA bunker and a radio. Ana and Goodwin take the radio to a higher elevation for a better signal. Ana tells Goodwin that she knows he is one of the "Others" because he was not on the plane, and they get in a fight, which ends in Goodwin's death. On the 41st day the group receives a radio transmission from the other group of survivors. However, Ana turns the radio off because she insists that the transmission came from the "Others." Ana, who is in despair at their situation, goes off by herself to cry, saying "This is our life now," as if there is no hope at all. Eko comes and comforts her and tells her everything will be all right. Ana Lucia asks Eko why he took forty days to talk, but he asks her why she took forty days to cry.

Sometimes our situation can seem completely hopeless. It may seem like no one can help us, and there's nothing we can do. The only thing we can do is cry and sulk about our misfortune. However, God has a plan for each one of us, and though it may seem like He is not in control, He uses our struggles to help build a stronger relationship with us. Even though we have struggles sometimes, God is always there in control. In the Bible, this is illustrated by the story of Job. Job is a very wealthy resident in the land of Uz. He does not let his riches go to his head, though. Job is a very righteous man, and he is thankful for all of the blessings that God has lavished on him. Satan then makes an appearance before God in heaven. God speaks about Job's great obedience and goodness. Satan believes that Job is only faithful because of his great riches. Satan says that if these blessings were taken away from Job, he would curse God. God allows Satan to challenge Job, by taking the things he loved. Job is so distraught but still refuses to curse God. He finds hope in God, even with his suffering. Some of Job's friends try to comfort their distressed friend, but he is not consoled by their attempts, believing that their claims dishonor God. A man named Elihu approaches Job soon after and expresses that God communicates with his people through suffering. When a person overcomes his suffering, he can then see the reparations and comfort that God has worked into his life. As God's people, we should rejoice in our suffering, because it brings clarity to God's beautiful comfort and the power that he has in all of our situations. Our suffering gives us an opportunity to seek God in the situation that we believe to be hopeless. Elihu greatly comforts Job in this hardship that occurred in his life. Job's distress was turned into peace in God. Although he lost everything he owned and had horrendous sores all over his entire body, he still praised God because he knew God had control of the situation. God was using this to shape Job, and Job was comforted in knowing that God had control of everything.

Psalm 18:2 says, "The LORD is my rock, my

fortress and my deliverer; my God is my rock, in whom I take refuge. He is my shield and the horn of my salvation, my stronghold." God watches over us and sees the big picture. He is always ready and able to deliver us. David also knows of God's comfort when everything seems hopeless: "The Lord is close to the brokenhearted and saves those who are crushed in spirit" (Psalm 34:18).

2 Corinthians 1:3-7 brings even more insight: Praise be to the God and Father of our Lord Jesus Christ, the Father of compassion and the God of all comfort, who comforts us in all our troubles, so that we can comfort those in any trouble with the comfort we ourselves receive from God. For just as we share abundantly in the sufferings of Christ, so also our comfort abounds through Christ. If we are distressed, it is for your comfort and salvation; if we are comforted, it is for your comfort, which produces in you patient endurance of the same sufferings we suffer. And our hope for you is firm, because we know that just as you share in our sufferings, so also you share in our comfort.

God allows us to go through tough times so we can

experience His comfort and so we know how to comfort others.

Finally, Jeremiah 29:11 gives light: "'For I know the plans I have for you,' declares the LORD, 'plans to prosper you and not to harm you, plans to give you hope and a future.'" God's plan gives hope.

What is something you are struggling with in your life right now? How do you deal with it?

_____

_____

_____

_____

When you are facing a hardship in life, what/who do you turn to for comfort?

_____

_____

_____

_____

Do you believe that God is in control of your situation? Why or why not?

_____

_____

_____

_____

How do you think He works through you?

_____

_____

_____

_____

What do you place your hope in?

_____

_____

_____

_____

The Tail End of the Story

"Although the world is full of suffering, it is full also of the overcoming of it." –Helen Keller

The Silent Victory

Episode 8
"Collision"

The episode starts out with Ana Lucia who recently returned to her job at the Los Angeles Police Department after being shot by a burglar while on call. Her mother, who is also the captain, lets her go back on patrol. While on patrol, Ana Lucia responds to a disturbance call and loses her temper. She pulls out her gun and aims it at the man who is trying to take the television. Her partner orders her to put her weapon away. Later, Ana Lucia finds out that the suspect, who shot her earlier, has been caught. His name is Jason McCormack. Ana Lucia is sent in to identify him so that he would be taken in. She looks at him and tells everyone that it's not him. Jason is soon released. Later, she sits in a bar and waits for Jason to leave. She follows him out and states that she was pregnant before she shoots him six times.

Later, on the Island, Sayid pulls his gun out on Ana Lucia after she shot Shannon. Sayid is knocked unconscious and tied to a tree. Libby and Michael tell them that Sawyer needs a doctor, otherwise he will not survive. Ana Lucia loses her temper and points her gun at Libby. A little later, Eko carries Sawyer away to find the other survivors. Michael gives Sayid water even though Ana Lucia might shoot him. Sayid starts to ask Michael questions about where he and his group came from. He tells Sayid about how Ana Lucia survived from the back of the plane and that the "Others" took Walt.

At the camp, Jack and Kate start to play a game of golf. While they were playing, they see Eko carrying Sawyer towards them. They go into the Hatch to help Sawyer. Meanwhile, Eko is exploring the hatch. He notices the DHARMA logo and sees a closet full of guns. He runs into Locke, and they stare at each other for a little while. Eko tells him that a girl was shot and killed. He described her as "tall with blonde hair." Locke finds out that the girl is Shannon. Locke asks Eko if he would take him to the scene, but Eko refuses. Jack tells Eko to take him to the scene. Jack then says, "Are you going to talk to me or are you just going to sit there?" Eko responds, "Anything I say will only make you angry, so yes, I will sit here." Suddenly, Michael runs into the Hatch and tells Jack what happened. Jack grabs a rifle and shotgun and makes his way out of the

Hatch. Then, Eko screams for him to stop. Jack tells him that he knows her and wants all of his people to be safe. Eko defends Ana Lucia and then agrees to take Jack to Sayid and to her if they do not bring any guns.

Eko's confrontation with Jack leads us right into the aspect of humans' defense mechanism and how we handle certain situations. Often, as humans in a fallen world, we become very quick to anger and sometimes lash out against others without considering the harm it will cause. God, however, has called us to be different from the others of this world. He desires us to approach every situation with a calm loving demeanor instead of deliberately causing anger. Paul says in Ephesians 4:29, "Do not let any unwholesome talk come out of your mouths, but only what is helpful for building others up according to their needs, that it may benefit those who listen." Eko knew that even if he tried to reason with Jack, it would only cause him to become angry, which would only make the situation worse for everyone. He avoided harsh words and a quarrel, even when it meant sitting quietly, not speaking a single word. Eko demonstrates what the Bible says in Proverbs 15:1, "A gentle answer turns away wrath, but a harsh word stirs up anger." He answered Jack calmly avoiding more conflict. Proverbs 29:11 points out, "Fools give full vent to their rage, but the wise bring calm in the end." Eko brought peace to turmoil.

We see this many times in the Bible, but one time in particular is the story of King David and the prophet Nathan. After becoming the king of Israel and being called "a man after God's own heart," David fell into temptation. One evening, as he was walking on the roof of his royal palace, David saw a woman bathing. He immediately thought she was extremely beautiful and was, at once, overcome by lust for her. He sent his messengers out to find her and bring her to his rooms at the palace, where he proceeded to lay with her. Soon after she returned home, David was sent word that she was pregnant. Not knowing what to do, David summoned her husband back from battle and tried to convince him to lie with his wife. His plan however did not work, and David eventually put her husband at the battlefront where he was killed. After a period of mourning, David took the woman, called Bath-Sheba, to be his wife. Soon after, God sent a prophet, named Nathan, to King David to tell him a story:

There were two men in a certain town, one rich and the other poor. The rich man had a very large number of sheep and cattle, but the poor man had nothing except one little ewe lamb he had bought. He raised it, and it grew up with him and his children. It shared his food, drank from his cup and even slept in his arms. It was like a daughter to him. Now a traveler came to the rich man, but the rich man refrained from taking one of his own sheep or cattle to prepare a meal for the traveler who had come to him. Instead, he took the ewe lamb that belonged to the poor man and prepared it for the one who had come to him" (2 Samuel 12:1-4).

This made David very angry and upset; he said the man who did these things, and took from the poor man, deserved to die. Nathan then proceeded to tell David that he was that man.

Nathan had every right to accuse David outright for the awful sins he had committed, but instead he took a calm approach, knowing that it would lead to a better outcome. He knew there was a better way of showing David what he had done, just as Eko knew that not stirring up anger in Jack would lead to a better result in the end. Remember James 1:19, "My dear brothers and sisters, take note of this: Everyone should be quick to listen, slow to speak and slow to become angry."

Has anybody wronged you in your life? Did it make you angry?

_____

_____

_____

_____

What did you do in return to that person? What should you have done?

_____

_____

_____

_____

What are three things you could do to avoid acting in a negative way?

_____

_____

_____

Pray to God, asking Him to help calm you in difficult situations:

Speak softly and carry a big stick.
–Theodore Roosevelt

Lost and Forgotten

Episode 9
"What Kate Did"

Sawyer, after being brought back from the other side of the island, lays in the hatch being tended to by Jack and Kate. Soon after, Kate goes into the jungle to collect fruit. On her way back, Kate sees something strange. Before her stands a black horse; this reminds her of her past and prompts memories to idle to the forefront of her mind. Coming back to the hatch, Kate then relieves Jack of his watch. Speaking to a deaf Sawyer and partly to herself, she tells Sawyer of the sighting of the horse. Halfway through her story, Sawyer then reaches up and grabs Kate saying, "You killed me. Why did you kill me?" Frightened Kate runs away leaving the hatch unmanned and Sawyer unattended

Meanwhile, Eko presents Locke with a Bible. After telling Locke the story of Josiah and what he found, he shows Locke what is actually inside the Bible. When opened, a hallowed out cavity is revealed, and Eko pulls out the missing reel from the reel found in the hatch. Will they finally get some answers about the island?

Later, Kate is again watching Sawyer, whom she believes to be channeling her dead father, and starts to talk to him again. She confesses to the murder of her assumed step-dad. Shortly after this, Sawyer wakes up and has heard the whole conversation. Kate and Sawyer head outside, and the black horse appears again. Seeking to confirm the sight, Kate looks to Sawyer who solemnly agrees. Back with Eko and Locke, the newfound clip is being played inside the hatch. In it, Dr. Candle reveals that the computer can be used to communicate with other people, but it is strongly advised that no one does this. The episode then ends with Michael staring at the computer screen as messages from Walt appear.

In Lost, all they knew was the island and the only truth they had about its existence, purpose, or function was from in the film reel. The reel was important because it gave them insights into the Island. In life, the Bible reveals to us the secrets of God. The Bible shows us what God is up to. It tells us why we were created and the purpose and plans of God. As the film reel tells the survivors of the purpose and function of the island, the entire Bible is vital to our understanding of the purpose and function of life.

When Locke is presented with the Bible, Eko tells a story that is quite relevant and interesting. This, of course, would be the tale of Josiah in 2 Kings 22. Josiah as a child, at the age of only eight years old, became king of Israel. Unlike recent previous kings, Josiah was a just ruler and set to rebuild the fallen temple. Little did Josiah know that what he would find among the ruins would be far greater than any rebuilt temple could offer. Hilkiah, the high priest, gave Josiah the Book of the Law. The Book of the Law contained the lost story of God and of His interaction with Israel. After hearing the history of his people and the faithfulness of God, Josiah resolved to keep a covenant with God. Josiah in the years ensuing followed the Lord's will. As 2 Kings 22:2 says, Josiah did "what was right in the eyes of the LORD and followed completely the ways of his father David, not turning aside to the right or to the left."

In our "brave, new world," we, like the Israelites of old, often forget or ignore God's word. We chose to disregard the life-giving and fulfilling words of God. Josiah, however, knew that the whole Bible is crucial to the understanding of life, love and our spirit. Without it, we are lost - adrift through life with no real meaning and purpose. While people and time come and go, there is only one lasting truth: the God of the Bible.

Do you feel as if you have a deep knowledge of the Bible?

_____

_____

_____

Do you find yourself ignoring certain parts of the Bible? Why?

_____

_____

_____

Do you feel you fully understand the Bible? If answered no, why not?

_____

_____

_____

Lost and Forgotten

"If you look for truth you may find comfort in the end; if you look for comfort you will not get either comfort or truth…" –C.S. Lewis

Confession Time

Episode 10
"The 23rd Psalm"

Boys are playing soccer when a band of insurgents pull up in a military style pickup truck. They grab a little boy trying to make him shoot a man in the head. He can't. His older brother, Eko, steps in and does it for him. The main insurgent takes off Eko's crucifix necklace and throws it on the ground, telling him that he "won't be needing this anymore," and takes him away. On the Island, Eko wants Charlie to take him to where he found the statue of Mary. They both know the statues are full of heroine. However, Eko also knows it will take him to the plane and his brother's body.

Continued flashbacks take us to Eko growing up and making a drug deal, as he seems to be an important insurgent now. He kills both of the drug dealers after they tell him that he does not have a soul. Later, Eko goes into a church where his younger brother is the priest. They discuss repentance, and Eko asks if his brother has forgotten how he got the crucifix around his neck (the same one that the insurgent threw on the ground). Some time later, Eko charges into his brother's church demanding him to reconsider his request to make him and his friend's priests so that they can fly drugs out of the country in the statues for an adequate cover. Eko tells his brother that they are both sinners now, and Eko's brother says that God will forgive him, implying he may not forgive Eko. The papers are signed. Eko is a priest, but complications occur when they try to leave in the plane. Eko's brother is shot.

What is the black smoke and why did it stop and run from Eko? Who is Michael communicating to on the computer? What do the verses (John 3:5; Acts 4:12; Romans 6:12; Revelation 5:3) mean on Eko's "Jesus stick?" Is this an episode of good son / bad son for both Charlie and Eko? How do both Eko and Charlie know Psalm 23? Although this episode keeps one wondering, it is clear about the need for confession and repentance. On one visit, Eko told his brother he came to give confession. His brother refused to hear it saying, "Why waste your time confessing; it won't help you." Eko questions, "It won't?" His brother says, "No, for confession to mean something it must have a penitent heart."

The priest rightly explains to Eko that a confession will not help him unless he has a repentant heart. In the book of Jonah, we see that Jonah was asked by God to go to the city of Nineveh to tell the people to turn away from their false gods and repent of their sins. Jonah was fearful of the people of Nineveh because of the gruesome way that they treated their enemies. Nineveh's society was built around warfare, stealing, and crime in general.

The city was known to be a hotbed for extortionists and murderers. For the neighboring countries, anytime they went to Nineveh, they lived in fear of becoming an enemy of the city. Therefore, Jonah had to learn to trust God before entering this dangerous place. His learning happened when he was running away from God. He tried to cross the sea away from Nineveh and was tossed from his boat and swallowed by a giant fish. After three days in the fish, he realized that no matter what, God is in control, and Jonah had to do what God wanted him to do - it was his calling. Learning from his experiences, Jonah went to Nineveh as a person that would stand out in the crowds because of what the acids inside the fish's stomach did to his skin. Even still, he was confident and trusted God fully. The first step to being forgiven is having a heart that is repentant and displays sorrow. It is evident in Jonah 3:10 (NIV):

> The Ninevites believed God. A fast was proclaimed, and all of them, from the greatest to the least, put on

sackcloth. When Jonah's warning reached the king of Nineveh, he rose from his throne, took off his royal robes, covered himself with sackcloth and sat down in the dust. This is the proclamation he issued in Nineveh: "By the decree of the king and his nobles: Do not let people or animals, herds or flocks, taste anything; do not let them eat or drink. But let people and animals be covered with sackcloth. Let everyone call urgently on God. Let them give up their evil ways and their violence. Who knows? God may yet relent and with compassion turn from his fierce anger so that we will not perish.

The people of Nineveh gave up everything they had, and turned their backs on all of their evil works to have hearts that were full of sorrow. One must be careful to not become jaded in a lifestyle that does not exhibit Godly attributes. This situation is explained in Ephesians 4:18: "They are darkened in their understanding and separated from the life of God because of the ignorance that is in them due to the hardening of their hearts." In order to have faith that one can be forgiven, one must trust God, and therefore, trust is a part of repentance. Repentance, in this sense, is the recognition that we are flawed, and realizing that God is in authority over us. We need Him to forgive us in order for us to move on to further a Godly mission. We are God's workmanship, and He calls us to do His work and glorify Him.

Bonnell Thornton said, "Some often repent, yet never reform; they resemble a man traveling in a dangerous path, who frequently starts and stops, but never turns back." True repentance isn't just an apology. It is reform. Matthew 12:41 says, "The men of Nineveh will stand up at the judgment with this generation and condemn it; for they repented at the preaching of Jonah, and now something greater than Jonah is here." Confession led to a change of heart and a change in actions. This is repentance. Repentance led to forgiveness which leads to a position blessed by God.

Do you trust God enough to admit to Him your deepest sins?

_____

_____

_____

_____

Do you trust God to take you where you need to go?

_____

_____

_____

_____

Can we admit to ourselves that we are flawed?

_____

_____

_____

_____

What changes need to be made in my life?

_____

_____

_____

_____

Confession Time

"Repentance is accepted remorse."
–Anna Sophia Swetchine

Who Is More Important

Episode 11
"The Hunting Party"

In this episode's flashback, we see Jack struggling once again. Constantly trying to fix those around him, Jack runs into trouble at his work and with his wife. Jack decides to do surgery on a high-risk patient against the wishes of Jack's dad, Christian. The man ends up dying after seven hours of surgery. Jack's marriage is also going poorly. He has been spending a great deal of time in the hospital, creating a rift in his marriage with Sarah. Sarah's pregnancy test came back negative, but she has no interest in talking to Jack about it. Jack tells Sarah he will put more effort into their marriage, but Sarah admits to have been having an affair with another man and walks out.

On the island, Jack wakes up in the Swan to find Locke unconscious in the armory and Michael with a gun to Jack's head. Michael locks both Jack and Locke up in the armory and goes off into the forest looking for Walt. When Kate and Sawyer arrive in the Swan, they find Jack and Locke and let them out, and then Jack, Sawyer, and Locke decide to go after Michael. Hurley spreads the word that Michael went looking for Walt, and when Jin finds out, he immediately starts to pack a bag to go help search for him. Sun tells him she doesn't want him to go, because she will worry like crazy about him, but Jin protests and says Michael is his friend. Sun replies that she is his wife, which convinces him to choose staying with her.

While arguing on whether or not Locke lost Michael's track, the bearded man from the raft interrupts them. The bearded man says that Walt is fine. Jack thinks that they outnumber the others when the bearded man says, "Light them up," and a ring of torches lights up around them. The bearded man then says, "Bring her out" to Alex, one of the others. Kate is brought out, gagged and bound. The bearded man gives them the option to give up the guns or Kate dies. Jack seems to be weighing the options very closely, but they eventually give the guns up. The episode ends back on the beach with Jack asking Ana Lucia if she was a cop, if she killed one of the others, and how long it would take to train an army.

Just like the situation with Sun and Jin, God also asks us to make a choice: a choice between Him and the world we inhabit. Although he knows it is a hard choice for any person to make, it is what He requires of us. He desires for us to turn our backs on this world and all the "fun" that may accompany it and live fully for Him. For the world as we know it now may look appealing and offer excitement and instant pleasure, but it is short-lived and leads to an unfulfilled life. By choosing God, your life on earth may seem more difficult, but you will always have Him by your side, loving you, protecting you, and calling you His own. Even after this short life, his love for you will continue to go on and you will get to spend eternity with him in the most perfect of all places.

One man who chose God over the world was named Paul. Paul was born and raised as a strict Jew and fully believed in the Jewish teachings. He even became a rabbi, or a Pharisee. When he first heard about the Christian beliefs, he thought that they were all lies. He, along with many other men, set out to get rid of this heresy, because it was a dangerous threat to the Jewish teachings, and they started persecuting the Christians. One day, on his way to Damascus to search for some Christians, Paul was blinded by a bright light and was laid prostrate in terror on the ground. A voice then spoke to him saying:

'Saul, Saul, why do you persecute me?' 'Who are you, Lord?' Saul asked. 'I am Jesus, whom you are persecuting,' he replied. 'Now get up and go into the city, and you will be told what you must do.'" The men who were with Paul led him into the city where he remained blind for three days. On the third day, a disciple named Ananias came to Paul to heal him of his blindness. Paul immediately could see and knew what his choice would be. He chose God. Paul saw the power of God and how he had intervened in his life and from that moment forward he gave his all to God; going from country to country proclaiming His name (Acts 7:58-8:1; Acts 9:1-19)

Paul, a man who persecuted Christians turned his life around completely. He turned his back on the sin of this world and went running toward a loving God who welcomed him. God loves every one of His sons and daughters, and He wants us to make the choice: choose Him.

Why is God important to you?

_____

_____

_____

_____

What in your life takes the number one importance? Could you give it up to follow God?

_____

_____

_____

_____

Pray to God, asking him to help you put Him first in your life.

A man can no more diminish God's glory by refusing to worship Him than a lunatic can put out the sun by scribbling the word, 'darkness' on the walls of his cell. –C.S. Lewis

God's Healing Water

Episode 12
"Fire + Water"

Episode twelve is a bit different than other episodes in that a lot of it does not actually happen. This episode centers on Charlie's heroin addiction and the problems that it causes. Much of this episode consists of flashbacks, dreams, and/or hallucinations. The flashbacks refer to Charlie's struggles with his brother and his brother's drug problems. The frustration of Drive Shaft failing, his piano being sold, and his lack of a sense of family have hurt him deeply. However, his nightmares and actions are what get him punched in the face. He dreams and feels he needs to save Aaron. He needs to save the baby. Charlie tries to explain everything to Mr. Eko, who interprets the dreams as possibly referring to baptism. Charlie starts a fire in order to steal Aaron and baptize him. It is interesting that fire was used in order to baptize Aaron and to save him from "The Unending Fire."

Claire first talks to Locke about baptism. Locke says, "Baptism is about making sure children get into Heaven should anything happen – it is spiritual insurance." Claire then talks to Eko. She is worried that if Aaron is baptized and something happens to them, that they won't be together. Eko explains that he can baptize both of them. The scene closes with Father Eko baptizing / sprinkling both Claire and Aaron.

Eko explains Jesus' baptism in a way that Christians do not agree with. This is likely due to the little Christian education he had received as explained in previous episodes. Christians understand that Jesus was sinless and therefore His baptism could not be for the cleansing of His sins.

Baptism causes a large amount of controversy among Christians. Eko portrays baptism as an act of desperation, in order to be saved before a person's death. Many different denominations have opposing views of this spiritual ritual. Some believe that it is completely necessary to get into heaven. Others think that it is simply a public declaration of one's faith. The Bible can be hard to interpret at times regarding the importance of baptism.

The first mention of baptism comes from the story of John the Baptist. John was leading a ministry preaching the coming of the Messiah. He said that all should repent and be baptized in preparation. People came from all over to confess their sins and be baptized by John. The story seems to point more to the public confession of sin rather than a necessary step for salvation.

However, this changes when Jesus meets with John the Baptist and requests to be baptized. John does not understand Jesus' motives and says that rather, he should be baptized by Jesus instead. Jesus insists, saying, "It is proper for us to do this to fulfill all righteousness," so John agreed and baptizes Him. When Jesus came out of the water, the heavens opened and the Spirit of God descended like a dove and came down upon him. A voice from heaven said, "This is my Son, whom I love; with him I am well pleased."

Jesus was and is completely without sin. Therefore, baptism did not have any repentance meaning for Him. This story points to a sort of completion of righteousness for Jesus. God's full approval Jesus was made quite evident. So in this context baptism seems to be more of a confession of faith.

This is echoed in Jesus' ministry. Jesus says in Mark 16:16, "Whoever believes and is baptized will be saved, but whoever does not believe will be condemned." So it seems that a confession of faith is necessary for salvation. Baptism does not give insurance for salvation in case of an early death as a baby. Many people believe in an age of accountability.

That is, babies are not old enough to distinguish right and wrong and therefore cannot be held accountable for their actions and sin. Therefore, baptism would be kind of pointless. In the episode, Claire also is baptized by Eko as Claire thinks that if only one of them is baptized, they will be separated if they both die. She implies that she believes in Christianity, but it is apparent that she does not know much about it. In her case, baptism may be meaningful, but only if she truly believes the message.

Jesus commands his disciples to practice baptism as well. Acts 22:16 says, "And now what are you waiting for? Get up, be baptized and wash your sins away, calling on his name." In the Great Commission, Jesus implies that baptism is crucial to salvation, however, whether by confession of faith or rather the importance of baptism itself is unclear. He says in Matthew 28:19-20, "Therefore go and make disciples of all nations, baptizing them in the name of the Father and of the Son and of the Holy Spirit, and teaching them to obey everything I have commanded you. And surely I am with you always, to the very end of the age." Baptism unifies the body of Christ, because we are all baptized as God's children in order to do His work. In Galatians 3:26-27 it says, "You are all sons of God through faith in Christ Jesus, for all of you who were baptized into Christ have clothed yourselves with Christ." Whether for salvation or testimony, one thing is sure: Christians are commanded to be baptized.

Do you believe baptism is required for salvation? Why or why not?

Have you ever been baptized?

Who will you talk to about baptism?

"Deep, unspeakable suffering may well be called a baptism, a regeneration, the initiation into a new state." –Ira Gershwin

Deceit from the Devil

Episode 13
"The Long Con"

In Episode 13, "The Long Con," the plot is all about the battle for power - it's about who controls the guns. Locke and Jack, who have assumed the leadership of the survivors, put all the guns in a locker and make a pact not to open it unless they both agree. However, when Sun is attacked by the Others, Jack decides to get the guns himself and build an army for the protection of the group. Locke disapproves of using the guns to build an army and turning to Sawyer for help, Locke decides to hide the guns. But things are not what they seem.

In the Sawyer-centered flashbacks set some years earlier, we learn about Sawyer's latest con of a troubled divorcée named Cassidy. Seemingly torn between completing the con and his feelings for Cassidy, Sawyer uses a string of deceptions to con her out of her money. In this episode, we see Sawyer use these same skills of deceptions to gain control of the guns. It was not the others who attacked Sun, but Charlie under the direction of Sawyer. Sawyer did this so that Jack and Locke would be against each other, and when Locke moves the guns, Sawyer follows him and takes the guns for himself. Now, as Sawyer says, "there's a new sheriff in town." At one point in this episode, Sawyer is confronted by Kate as to why he took advantage of the group, especially when the people started liking him. He said to her, "You run. I con. A tiger don't change their stripes."

Essentially sin is rooted in deception. It involves some level of compromise with the truth, from obvious lies to the subtle deception of pride, seeing ourselves as better than or more important than we are. We are enticed by something that appears to be what it really is not.

The fingers of deception can be seen in practically every major character and incident in the book of Genesis. Through deceit, the characters in Genesis try to carve out a future apart from the promises of God, like Abraham when he tries to save his own neck, passes off Sarah as his sister (Genesis 20:2) or Jacob when he pretends to be his brother to steal his blessing (Genesis 27). Despite the deceit all throughout Genesis, God proves Himself to be powerful to bring truth and fulfillment out of the deceptive situation. God is truth and through the truth, God shows Himself to be in control. God's truth-is more powerful than man's lies.

Not only does deception allow us to see the nature of sin and of God's control, it also sheds light on the grace of God. Repeatedly Genesis illustrates that you don't have to be perfect for God to work through you. Even though Abraham's decedents are continually deceptive, God works through them and redeems them out of their deception. He even chose to use Jacob despite the fact that Jacob's name meant "he grasps the heel" or figuratively "he deceives" (Genesis 25:6; 27:36). God eventually redeems him and renames him "Israel" meaning "he struggles with God" (Genesis 32:28). The true Israelite, the true child of God, has of course been redeemed from deception. God shows Himself to be the God who consistently keeps His promises, rescuing his people from the destructiveness of their own deceptions by the power of His truth.

Sawyer just can't seem to break away from his evil ways. He refuses to turn away from his deceit. Like Jeremiah 8:5 says, "Why, then, has this people turned away in perpetual backsliding? They hold fast to deceit; they refuse to return." But we do not have to be this way. We do not have to live in guilt and sin. God is our saving grace when we are conned by the world and the deceptiveness of evil. He is powerful enough to break us out of the cycle of evil. God calls us to turn away from sin and deceit of the devil. He offers us redemption and saving grace.

Can lying ever be good? Why or why not?

_____

_____

_____

_____

_____

_____

Do you like it when people lie to you just to make you feel better or so you won't get mad?

_____

_____

_____

_____

_____

What items in life do most consider "little white lies?" Do you agree?

_____

_____

_____

_____

_____

_____

Who lies for you will lie against you.
                                        −Bosnian Proverb

The Whole Truth, and Nothing but

Episode 14
"One of Them"

Truth: what is it, what does it mean, and how can I find it? The episode opens with a flashback containing various explosions, and many Arabs scrambling to destroy documents. In fact, they are destroying the truth. While this is happening, American soldiers break in and order them to stop, and get on the ground. They ask who the commanding officer is, but the Iraqis don't seem to understand. Eventually, Sayid speaks up and says that there is no commanding officer present. It is soon revealed that this was a lie. Later, Sayid is forced to torture his commanding officer to get some information from him.

Back on the Island, Danielle has captured a man claiming to be Henry Gale in a trap. Sayid cuts him down, and Danielle shoots Henry in the shoulder with an arrow saying that he is "one of them." She follows this up by saying, "for a long time, he will lie." Sayid carries Henry into the hatch; Jack removes the arrow, dresses the wound, and puts him in the armory. Without

Jack's knowledge, Locke changes the combination to the armory, and when they move Henry into the armory, Sayid locks himself in with Henry.

Sayid does not believe that Henry is who he says he is, but thinks he is one of the "others." Torture ensues, much to Jack's displeasure. Locke and Jack are outside listening to Henry being beaten by Sayid. Jack is completely against it, and says to Locke, "What if he's telling the truth?" Locke replies with a simple, "What if he's not?"

In the midst of filtering truth from the lies, Sawyer is trying to find a tree frog. This humorous display has him find Hurley hiding food. Like the rest, Hurley lies. He says he doesn't have anything. Sawyer says, "Wipe the nothing on your chin." It can be embarrassing to get caught in a lie.

As Christians, deciphering the truth is one of the hardest things to do. We are confronted with what to believe either from our peers, our parents, or from a higher, more sinister power. Since the early days of the earth, finding out what is true has been a huge trip-up for humans. Half-truths are the worst of all!

Satan is very accomplished at weaving truth into lies to get humans to falter. The first instance of this is in the Garden of Eden. He takes what God said about the tree of the knowledge of good and evil, and puts a different twist on it. Genesis 3:1-4 record,

> Now the serpent was more crafty than any of the wild animals the LORD God had made. He said to the woman, 'Did God really say, 'You must not eat from any tree in the garden'?' The woman said to the serpent, 'We may eat fruit from the trees in the garden, but God did say, 'You must not eat fruit from the tree that is in the middle of the garden, and you must not touch it, or you will die.' 'You will not certainly die,' the serpent said to the woman. 'For God knows that when you eat from it your eyes will be opened, and you will be like God, knowing good and evil.'

Satan is crafty. He changes God's words and soon even Eve added to God's words by saying that they couldn't even touch the fruit. Later, Satan outright says God is lying. He says that partaking in the fruit will turn Adam and Eve into beings just like God. Clearly, this is false, as they were kicked out of the garden. This initial sin led to a fallen creation.

Even Jesus was confronted with this problem. Jesus was fasting and in the desert for forty days. The

Bible says that He was hungry. Satan came to Jesus, offering Him many things if Jesus would but bow down to him. He said many things that align with Scripture, but took them out of context with misinterpretation. Jesus responded with a clear interpretation of Scripture, and his knowledge of the heart of God (Matthew 4:1-11). The beauty of John 8:32 is realized, "Then you will know the truth, and the truth will set you free." Truth wins. Those who are truthful, win.

It is worth noting that as a child, "And Jesus grew in wisdom and stature, and in favor with God and man" (Luke 2:52). Jesus studied the Scriptures, and He too grew in wisdom. Christians need to study God's Word regularly so they are ready when the crossroads bring a difficult choice between which way is paved in truth. 2 Timothy 2:15 says, "Do your best to present yourself to God as one approved, a worker who does not need to be ashamed and who correctly handles the word of truth." Christians need to study the Word so they aren't ashamed by being caught in a lie or tricked by false statements.

Truth: what is it, what does it mean, and how can I find it? Look at what the Bible says. Compare it with life's situations. It is relevant for today. Many times, confrontation will arise, and what seems like truth, will be all lies. Remember: "Sanctify them by the truth; your word is truth" (John 17:17). God's Word is truth!

How does one figure out what is true, and what is false?

_____

_____

_____

_____

_____

How do you search for truth?

_____

_____

_____

_____

_____

_____

Is there a falsehood you need to personally correct? How? When?

"...God offers to every mind its choice between truth and repose. Take which you please. You can never have both." –Ralph Waldo Emerson

The Greatest Sacrifice

Episode 15
"Maternity Leave"

Claire is in a panic, because her baby Aaron is sick. Jack says that it is just a fever, but Clair is convinced it's something more. During this episode, Claire keeps having jumbled flashbacks to when she was captured by the others. With the help of Libby, she begins to put pieces of memories together from when she was captured by the others. Convinced that the Others infected her baby with a sickness, Clair enlisted the help of Kate to find Rousseau. Clair is convinced that Rousseau can help find the "antidote." Together, Claire, Kate and Rousseau find and explore the DARMA station where Claire was "treated." Unfortunately the bunker has been cleaned out.

This whole time, Claire believed that Rousseau had been out to hurt her, that she had been against her. But when Claire notices a scratch on Rousseau's arm and has another flashback, things start to piece back together in her mind. She realizes that Rousseau was never trying to hurt her, but to save her. When Claire and Kate get back to camp Jack takes another look at Aaron; thankfully his fever is gone.

Back in the hatch, Jack and Locke are still unsure of what to do with their prisoner, Henry. Eko believes that he has something to do with the Others and even asks him forgiveness for killing two Others. Henry starts playing mind games with Locke about who is in charge. Henry implies that Jack is making all the calls and that Locke is just his shadow. Locke says that the decisions are mutual but leaves the room obviously frustrated.

A part of the episode that really sticks out is when Rousseau says, "I hope your baby is not infected. But if he is, I hope you know what must be done." Rousseau doesn't say exactly "what must be done," but we know what this means. It means that if the baby is infected with something that should be quarantined, the baby has to be killed so that other people may live. One life must be sacrificed to save the lives of everyone else.

For Rousseau, this idea is self-serving. Someone else must be sacrificed so that she can save herself. This is the exact same idea that the Jewish religious leaders had when dealing with Jesus. In John 11, Mary and her sister Martha sent word to Jesus that their brother Lazarus was sick. Jesus begins to make his way to Lazarus, but it was too late. When Jesus arrives, Lazarus has been in the tomb for four days already.

Jesus heads over to the tomb, and he tells Lazarus to come out. Then Lazarus got up and came out of the tomb wearing his grave clothes.

Because of this miracle, the Jewish religious leaders were worried that the people would start believing in Jesus. If this happened, they would lose their power and positions in the culture. Thinking of themselves they plot to kill Jesus. During this discussion, the high priest Caiaphas said, "You do not realize that it is better for you that one man die for the people than that the whole nation perish." (John 11:49) This is the same selfish idea Rousseau had; someone else must die so that we can save ourselves.

As Jesus continually did in His life, He took a worldly philosophy and turned it upside down for his Kingdom. 1 Thessalonians 5:10 (emphasis added) says, "He died for us so that... we may live together with him." Jesus, in the ultimate act of love for others, sacrificed himself so that others could live. After the fall of man, we are all naturally sinners. We all fall short. We all sin, over and over and over again. We also know that "the wages of sin is death" (Romans 6:23). We deserve to be separated from God for eternity. We are already sick and already infected. We deserve to be quarantined. But take heart, because we have a loving and gracious Savior. He knew that we could not save ourselves. He loved us so much that He was willing to sacrifice His own life so that we could be saved. Christ died for us so that we may live. Alone we would die of our sickness unable to save ourselves; but in Christ we live. The price has been paid.

Would you be willing to sacrifice anything to save many people?

___

___

___

___

___

Do you think that because Jesus died for us that we should live our lives for Him?

___

___

___

___

___

Have you ever had to sacrifice something for the benefit of others?

_____

_____

_____

_____

_____

_____

"Two roads diverged in a wood, and I--I took the one less traveled by, And that has made all the difference."
–Robert Frost

Fixing Our Mistakes

Episode 16
"The Whole Truth"

Sun is working in her garden when Jin bursts through the bushes. He destroys her garden. He is scared for her since her kidnapping. Later we see Sun is feeling sick. She wonders if she is pregnant; she approaches Sawyer and asks for a pregnancy test. Jack confirms that she is pregnant. Sun does not immediately tell Jin.

Locke asks Anna Lucia to interrogate Henry Gale, who is possibly one of the "Others." Sayid and Jack were unable to get any information out of him, so Locke asks Anna Lucia to give it a shot. She is able to get Henry to draw a map to where his balloon is supposedly located. She does not tell Jack or Locke, but instead tells Sayid and Charlie. The three of them go into the jungle to search for Henry's alleged balloon; it's a day's walk from the camp.

Later, Jin is in Sun's garden, replanting everything he tore up. Sun appears and asks what he is doing. Jin tells her, "I'm fixing a mistake." She says that he didn't have to, but he says, "Yes, I did." Sun then tells him that she is pregnant, and Jin says that it must be a miracle.

Jin realized he needed to fix a mistake. He didn't just say he was sorry, but he did something. This episode has at least two other situations where someone fixed a mistake. First, in a flashback, Dr. Kim approaches Sun and tells her he lied. He was afraid of Jin, so he said that it was physically her fault they couldn't have children when actually Jin was infertile. He intentionally lied and tried to fix the mistake with the truth. Second, Ana Lucia apologizes to Sayid for killing Shannon. Although it was an accident, she was right in trying to smooth the waters.

When Jesus entered Jericho there was a man named Zacchaeus, a very wealthy chief tax collector. Zacchaeus wanted to see Jesus, but because of the large crowd and his small stature, he climbed into a nearby Sycamore tree in order to get a better view. Jesus drew nearer and approached the tree Zacchaeus was occupying. He told Zacchaeus that He would be staying with him in his house. Zacchaeus welcomed him, but the crowd complained because Zacchaeus was a sinner and had cheated people out of their money. Zacchaeus stopped and told Jesus that he would give away half of his possessions to the poor, and anyone who he had unfairly taken money from he would pay back them back four times what he had taken. Zacchaeus may have been a little man, but he took huge strides in trying to fix his mistakes. He didn't just repay people - he took a loss. His actions conveyed a heart that was truly sorry.

Zacchaeus repented of his sin, promising to give away half of everything he owned, and to pay back four times what he had taken. Zacchaeus was fixing his mistakes, repenting of his sin. In the episode, "The Whole Truth," Jin tears apart Sun's garden out of fear and anger, but by the end of the episode, he is back in her garden, replanting what he destroyed - fixing his mistake. Proverbs 24:16 says, "For though the righteous fall seven times, they rise again, but the wicked stumble when calamity strikes." Even when one falls or fails, he need to rise up and correct it. Likewise, in his letter to the church in Philippi, Paul says, "Not that I have already obtained all this, or have already arrived at my goal, but I press on to take hold of that for which Christ Jesus took hold of me" (Philippians 3:12). Not even Paul went through life without having to fix his own mistakes.

As Christians, we are called to help others stay away from sin and to help them recover. However, before we can help others, we have to repent of our own sin and fix our mistakes. We don't want to be seen

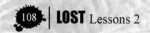

as trying to clear a speck out of someone else's eye when we have a tree stump in our own eye.

Paul gives great advice in Ephesians 4:26 when he says. "In your anger do not sin: Do not let the sun go down while you are still angry." Mistakes need to be corrected immediately. They should be fixed on the same day if at all possible. Letting mistakes linger can allow other mistakes to stew inside. This makes the mistake even greater. Mistakes, whether intentional or accidental, need attention. When Jin fixed his mistake, Sun could not hold back her emotions as she said, "I love you." This was clearly a fresh start.

List some mistakes you have made?

_____

_____

_____

What are some ways to fix the mistakes?

_____

_____

_____

_____

How can we avoid making the same mistakes in the future?

_____

_____

_____

Think of other Biblical examples of people repenting of their sin?

_____

_____

_____

"All men make mistakes, but only wise men learn from them." –Winston Churchill

Light of the World

Episode 17
"Lockdown"

"Lockdown" is literally Locke down in two ways. First, in flashbacks, Locke goes to his father's funeral only to find out later he faked his death. He scammed 2 men out of $700,000 and wanted Locke to help. Locke meets him only to have Helen show up. In her anger and his despair, he drops to a knee to propose only to be rejected. Locke is emotionally "Locke down." Second, Locke is down physically. In the hatch, he gets trapped under a retractable door. Henry Gale has to help him. When Henry is out of the room, the lighting in the room changes to black lighting which in turn reveals a secret map on the wall. After a few moments, the black lights turn off and the map disappears.

The other characters are involved in seeing if someone is bluffing. Hurley, Sawyer, Kate and Jack play poker. Jack wins. Ana Lucia, Charlie and Sayid look for a hot air balloon to see if Henry is bluffing. Sayid even digs up a grave. Henry loses. It is interesting that in an episode that centers around two graves, neither have the body of the one people are told.

During the lockdown when Locke was pinned

underneath the blast doors, he looked at the door under normal light and saw nothing unique. However, all of a sudden, the black light turned on revealing a map of grand proportions. Locke knew that this must mean something. One could take from this scene that people look into different "lights" to guide their way and reveal the map of their existence. As Christians, we can see that there is only one true Light that is worth following. In 1 Kings 18:21, Scripture says, "Elijah went before the people and said, 'How long will you waver between two opinions? If the LORD is God, follow him; but if Baal is God, follow him.' But the people said nothing." No response. A choice had to be made. Verses 22-24 continue,

> Then Elijah said to them, 'I am the only one of the LORD's prophets left, but Baal has four hundred and fifty prophets. Get two bulls for us. Let Baal's prophets choose one for themselves, and let them cut it into pieces and put it on the wood but not set fire to it. I will prepare the other bull and put it on the wood but not set fire to it. Then you call on the name of your god, and I will call on the name of the LORD. The god who answers by fire—he is God.

The people stood there not knowing which God to put their faith in and fully trust. The prophets of Baal then summoned upon their god and nothing happened. Then it was Elijah's turn. Elijah ordered that four large jars full of water be poured onto the altar three times. He prayed to God for fire to come down and consume the altar. God answered with a mighty flame that came down from heaven and literally burned everything up until it was no more. The stones and the soil were even melted. This even shows a couple of points. First, to believe more than one thing is to believe nothing. One must choose one way and stick to it. One cannot play on both teams. A side needs to be chosen. Second, to choose anything isn't enough. One must find truth and follow it.

There are many views of God, and they cannot all be right. Every view of God will conflict at some point; we must find the way that does not have any contradictions. Jesus tells us in John 14:6 that that way is Jesus Himself, "Jesus answered, 'I am the way and the truth and the life. No one comes to the Father except through me.'" We can see that Christ Himself prepares the way for us to get to heaven.

Locke noticed that looking in different lights brought different scenes. Only one kind brought the map, truth, and direction. In John 8:12 Jesus says, "When Jesus spoke again to the people, he said, 'I am the light of the world. Whoever follows me will never walk in darkness, but will have the light of life.'" Jesus is the Light we need. John 3:19 explains why most refuse this Light: "This is the verdict: Light has come into the world, but people loved darkness instead of light because their deeds were evil." People want to follow themselves, so they ignore the Light. They hide in darkness.

Is there any part of your life that you are hiding from God?

_____

_____

_____

Why won't people fully follow Jesus?

_____

_____

_____

What steps will you take to live in the Light?

_____

_____

_____

_____

_____

"One must keep on pointing out that Christianity is a statement which, if false, is of no importance, and if true, of infinite importance. The one thing it cannot be is moderately important." –C.S. Lewis

To Eat or Not to Eat

Episode 18
"Dave"

After many weeks on the island, Hurley is still struggling with his incessant desire to consume as much food as possible. He is, however, getting a lot of help from Libby who is doing everything in her power to break Hurley of his obsession with food and get him healthy. She has such a positive influence on him that together they destroy Hurley's secret stash of food.

Throughout a series of flashbacks, we learn that Hurley has not always listened to the good influences in his life. During Hurley's stay in the mental hospital, he had a friend named Dave. Every scene that Dave is in, he is trying to persuade Hurley to take some unhealthy food or to escape from the hospital. Dave is constantly drawing Hurley away from what he knows is right.

Back on the island, mysteriously Dave shows up in the woods and again tries lead Hurley astray. He claims that Hurley is in a coma and is still at the hospital and leads Hurley to a cliff and says the only way to wake up is to jump off, then Dave jumps off the cliff himself. Hurley is looking down after him trying to decide what to do when Libby comes up and asks what he is doing. They begin to discuss whether or not this is all fake. After a great deal of coaxing and a kiss, Libby convinces Hurley that she, the island, and all of his experiences are real. Relief swoops over Hurley as they walk away hand in hand.

Like Hurley, we all have to deal with many different influences in our lives. We are constantly being told different things from all different directions. We hear one thing at school, one at church, another with our parents, another from TV, and still another from our friends.

In 1 Kings 21, King Ahab must decide between the influences in his life. The King desires a vineyard in his garden, but discovers that he cannot have it. His wife, Jezebel, questions his authority and tells him that he should have taken the vineyard. She thinks he should just have the owner killed in order to have Ahab get the vineyard. But Elijah, a prophet from God, brings a very different message: do what is right or suffer the consequences. The King had a choice: who do I listen to?

As Christians, our success in fighting for God's kingdom is dependent upon being ability to filter the truth of God from the lies of Satan. Every day we are bombarded with all types of information, while some of it is true, much of it is false and many times it's difficult to discern what is right and wrong. That's why Paul warns us in Colossians 2:8, "See to it that no one takes you captive through hollow and deceptive philosophy, which depends on human tradition and the elemental spiritual forces of this world rather than on Christ."

If we let them, the influences of evil will get into our minds and cause us to make horrible choices that will lead us to be ineffective for Christ. 1 Peter 5:8 reminds us to, "Be self-controlled and alert. Your enemy the devil prowls around like a roaring lion looking for someone to devour." We need to make sure that we are prepared to see through the lies and bad influences in our lives. We need to train to know God's truth and allow His truth to sink into our hearts and our lives so that we can be effective servants of God's kingdom.

Is the momentary "rush" worth the final consequences?

_____

_____

_____

_____

Is it ever worth disappointing God?

How do we avoid getting deceived by the wrong influences?

"Nobody ever did, or ever will, escape the consequences of his choices." –Alfred A. Montapert

Be Still

Episode 19
"S.O.S"

Episode 19 focuses mainly on Rose and Bernard. During their flashbacks, Rose first meets Bernard when she is trying to get her car out of the snow. Later, Rose and Bernard have a nice dinner at Niagara Falls. Bernard proposes. Rose tells him that she is dying, but she does say yes. Next they are in Australia for their honeymoon. Bernard brought them there because he found a "doctor" to heal Rose. The doctor says by channeling energy, he can heal her. But after looking at her, he says that he cannot save her. Rose tells the doctor to tell Bernard that she was healed, so that he won't keep worrying about her.

Meanwhile on the Island, Bernard wants to do everything he can do get off the Island. He doesn't understand why people are getting used to being on the Island. He wants out, so He decides to make a huge S.O.S. in the sand, hoping that someone will see, and eventually help them. After some time, the group of people that were helping Bernard quit making the sign with Bernard. Bernard complains to Rose, but Rose isn't very sympathetic. Then Bernard tells Rose that if it wasn't for him, then she would have not been healed. Bernard seems to always looking for ways to change things or make things better. Later, Locke and Rose are talking and reference his crutches. Rose reassures him that he will be healed quite quickly. She says that because she has been healed on the Island, and John was already, too.

Also on the Island, Jack decides to go find the "Others" to trade "Henry" for Walt. He brings Kate with him. They get caught in a trap, but escape. They go to where they met the "Others" earlier, and Jack starts shouting for them to reveal themselves. They decide to spend the night at the line they were not supposed to cross, and the episode finishes with Michael running towards them, and he passes out in Kate's arms.

If we focus on Bernard, we find that he is always trying to fix things. When he finds that Rose is sick, he takes it on as his responsibility to get her healed. He does everything he possibly can to get her healed. He even goes as far as taking her to Australia to see one of those crazy "healer" doctors. Bernard's problem is that he can't just let things be. He feels he needs to get up, go out, do something, fix something or even fix someone.

There is a common misconception that to serve

God, you have to go somewhere crazy or far away. Some people think that the only way to serve God is by mission trips to South America or building wells in Uganda. Both of which are good things, but these are not the only ways to serve God. An incredible thing about our Father is that He can use you and I where we are at this moment. You can hardly find a better illustration of this than the story of Paul and the jailer.

Acts 16 tells us of a slave girl who made her owners rich by predicting the future for people. This little girl was not the one actual predicting the future, because she was possessed. This fortune teller went around following Paul and yelling things day after day. Finally, Paul got fed up with this and said to the spirit possessing the girl; "In the name of Jesus Christ I command you to come out of her!"(Acts 16:18). After this event, which was essentially an exorcism, the slave girl had no more abilities to see or predict people's future. When the owners of this slave girl learned of this, they realized that she would be bringing in a lot less money from then on. The owner dragged Paul and his friend Silas to the marketplace in the town and convinced everyone that they were throwing the city into an uproar. This was an utterly false accusation, but, nonetheless, Paul and Silas were stripped naked and beaten. Then, to add insult to injury, they were thrown in jail. Not only were they thrown in a cell, they were put in the inner cell, and their feet were fastened to the stocks. Paul and Silas weren't going anywhere.

What is so incredible about this story is what Paul and Silas do afterwards. Most people, after this experience, would not be thrilled. But Paul and Barnabas are totally content. In fact, late into the night they were praying and singing hymns to God. The other prisoners listened. In the most unlikely place, God used Paul and Silas to spread the word about Himself. Paul did not have to get up, go somewhere or do something to serve God. He did it from a jail cell.

But the story goes on. While Paul and Silas are singing, an earthquake breaks loose, and the prison doors happen to open and the prisoners' chains break loose. When the jailer wakes up he sees the prison doors open and he tries to kill himself; most likely because he knows that he will be killed anyway for letting them escape. Paul tells him to calm down and that none of the prisoners have left. The jailer comes to Paul trembling and asks how he can be saved. The jailer accepts Christ and eventually his whole family does, too.

Bernard feels like he has to go somewhere. He

has to go to Australia to fix Rose. He has to labor over a sign in the sand to get off the Island. What Bernard needs more than any of these things is to be content. Psalm 46:10 reads, "Be still and know that I am God." We need to be still. We need to quit running around looking for trivial, insignificant things to do because God likely has a simple plan for us. God's plan for Paul was to pray and sing like he would anywhere else and that led to people being saved. Building wells in Ethiopia and going on mission trips anywhere are very good things. But they may not be your things. God put you where you are for a reason. Serve Him where you are. You don't need to go anywhere unless He tells you to. Listen. Be Still.

While at Niagara Falls, Rose asks Bernard a very life summarizing question, "So what does God have to do to get your attention?" God shouldn't have to take us somewhere to get our attention. We can and should see Him daily where we are.

Do you ever question God's plan for you?

_____

_____

_____

What does God have to do to get your attention?

_____

_____

_____

_____

How does God make Himself obvious in your life?

_____

_____

_____

_____

What can you do where you are now to serve God?

_____

_____

_____

_____

_____

"You are never in the wrong place to serve God... Bloom where you are planted."–Pastor Michael Eaton

Courage Against Revenge

Episode 20
"Two for the Road"

Ana Lucia doesn't forgive and forget. In the midst of Michael being brought back to camp and Hurley preparing a picnic for Libby, there is the past and present life of Ana Lucia. The episode starts with Ana Lucia and her mother standing over Jason's dead body at the city morgue. A disagreement and guilt lead to Ana Lucia quitting as a police officer and taking the job in security at the airport. She becomes "Tom's" body guard in Sydney, Australia. Later she calls her mom letting her know she is sorry and wants to come home. On the Island, Ana Lucia is almost killed by Henry. She seduces Sawyer to get a gun. In the hatch, Michael finally wakes up and John and Jack decide to go get the guns back from Sawyer. Ana Lucia stays to take care of Michael. While she is in the hatch, she loads the gun she stole from Sawyer and goes to Henry. Michael comes out and Ana Lucia tells him that she couldn't shoot Henry, so Michael offers to do it for her. Instead, Michael shoots Ana Lucia and then shoots Libby when she surprises him. He then shoots himself in the arm.

Ana Lucia's desire for revenge killed her. The only reason she was on Flight 815 was the fact that she was running from her past since she took revenge on Jason. The only way she got shot was she gave the gun to Michael hoping for revenge on Henry. Forgiveness takes more courage than revenge.

Imagine having your own family beat you, throw you into a pit and leave you to die. They do have a change of heart and come back but only to sell you into slavery. You spend years in prison. Most people would give up, and spend their days wallowing in self pity. But Joseph didn't. His courage and faith in God kept him and enabled him to do great things.

Joseph was the 11th son of Jacob and the first child of Rachel. Because he was the child that his father favored most, the rest of his brothers hated him. He would often tell of the dreams he had of his brothers and parents bowing down to him. This only angered his brothers further. Eventually they had had enough of Joseph and threw him into a pit and intended to leave him for dead. One of the brothers talked them out of this plan and convinced them to sell Joseph into slavery instead. After many trials and years in prison, Joseph was appointed a position of high power in Egypt by the Pharaoh for interpreting a dream for him. Because of the dream, Pharaoh and Joseph were informed of a famine to come, so they started filling their storehouses with grain for the people of Egypt. When the famine came, people from all around came to Egypt in search of food. Among those who came were Joseph's brothers. Joseph, now being in a position of power, could take revenge on his brothers for how they had treated him, but instead he forgives them and takes them into his home. Genesis 50:19-21 records the climax in the situation: " But Joseph said to them, 'Don't be afraid. Am I in the place of God? You intended to harm me, but God intended it for good to accomplish what is now being done, the saving of many lives. So then, don't be afraid. I will provide for you and your children.' And he reassured them and spoke kindly to them." Joseph doesn't take revenge, he forgives his brothers- he speaks kindly to them and he views God as blessing him.

Though his brothers had meant him harm, God meant good things for Joseph. It probably didn't look that way to Joseph sometimes, but he persevered through his hardships and learned humility. Unlike Ana Lucia, Joseph faced his challenges courageously. The evidence of his courage is in his behavior, doing right even when he was wronged. He learned to wait patiently on God and to look to God for everything. It takes tremendous courage to look away from circumstance and look instead to God. A good part of faith is having the courage to believe despite all that we see. This is how God wants us to approach the hard situations in our life, gracefully and with faith; rather than rant against them, He wants us to make the best of our situations and rely on Him to care for us.

Leviticus 19:18 speaks a common theme in Scripture, "Do not seek revenge or bear a grudge against anyone among your people, but love your neighbor as yourself. I am the LORD." Revenge, or punishment based on accurate and fair judgment, is God's position, not ours. Romans 12:19 continues the theme, "Do not take revenge, my dear friends, but leave room for God's wrath, for it is written: 'It is mine to avenge; I will repay,' says the Lord."

Interesting side note: Henry mentions to Locke that the "man in charge – great man, but not forgiving man." Although revenge may be sweet, one normally appreciates the fact that the real "Man in Charge" is a forgiving God. Forgiveness takes more courage than revenge.

Courage Against Revenge

What type of situations have you been put in where you wanted to take revenge?

_____

_____

_____

_____

_____

_____

How did you go about the situation, did you take revenge or not?

_____

_____

_____

_____

_____

_____

What can you do to help out in your struggles and learn how not to take revenge but trust in God?

Courage Against Revenge

"A man that studieth revenge keeps his own wounds green, which otherwise would heal and do well."
—Anonymous

What is God's Plan?

Episode 21
"?"

Episode twenty-one begins with Eko having a dream where Ana Lucia (who was recently shot and killed) appears to him and questions him about the church he is building. She informs him that he has to help John. Eko's dream begins to turn into a group of flashbacks, many including his brother, Yemi. He tells Eko that he needs to make John show him the question mark. Yemi says, "John will not want to show you, so you must make him." Eko immediately puts this dream into action. He grabs an axe, which his brother told him to bring, and goes to find John.

The episode then goes back to Jack, Sawyer, Kate, and John walking through the jungle. All of a sudden, Michael pretends to fall out of the hatch, claiming that Henry Gale shot him and ran. They find Ana Lucia dead and Libby nearly dead on the ground. Eko offers to follow the trail of Henry Gale, along with John.

Eko has another flashback to when he was supposedly a priest at his brother's church, where a miracle occurs. A little girl has supposedly been revived from death. The little girl had drowned and stopped breathing, but during the autopsy, they cut her open, and she woke up and began screaming. The doctor who was performing the surgery even had the autopsy on tape, which he plays to Eko. Eko eventually meets this teenage girl, but her parents will not let him talk to her. She shows up at the airport before his flight leaves, and tells him not to go through with his travels. She said his brother appeared to her in a dream, and told her to tell him that.

Eko and Locke are walking in the jungle, when Locke realizes that Eko really is not after Henry Gale. Eko explains to John how they have to find the "question mark." Eko has another dream, where Yemi leads him up a cliff that he and John are camping by. Eko knows he needs to climb the cliff in order to find the "question mark." The next day he climbs up and looks out to find that the question mark is, indeed, there. The two find the plane that Yemi had crashed in, and find another hatch under the wing. In this hatch they find screens and another informational tape from Dharma. The screens in the hatch are connected to their own hatch, and they can watch everything that their group is doing. They also find a bunch of notebooks with information about other peoples' stay in this hatch. The video commands the occupants of the hatch to observe, study and report everything that happens inside the first hatch. This orientation film implies that "pushing the button" is merely a psychological experiment that has no meaning. After it ends, Eko begins collecting the paperwork saying that it could be useful. Locke just sits there and wonders why Eko is doing anything after seeing that video. John tries to convince Eko that pushing the button is now pointless and they shouldn't worry about it. Eko counters however, and believes that what they are doing is now more important than ever.

Eko believes that he is meant to find the question mark. After finding the new hatch and watching the tape, he believes that he is now meant to push the button when no one else will. Eko feels a pull towards goals whether though dreams or just gut feeling. Eko's story is very similar to the story of King Josiah in 2 Kings 22-23:30. Oddly enough, this same story is mentioned earlier in episode 09, "What Kate Did," when Eko tells Locke about the Bible they found inside the tail-section survivor's hatch.

To recap, Josiah inherited the throne at only eight years old. At this time, a series of terrible kings had ruled Israel, including his own father. The people were not obeying God and righteousness had been lost years ago. Josiah saw all this wickedness but stayed true to the Lord's will. After ruling eighteen years, Josiah felt that he was meant to repair the now dilapidated Temple. He sent his secretary who was given a forgotten text by the high-priest there. It was the Book of the Law. Josiah had the book read to him and tore his robes after seeing how these laws had been broken by the people and ignored by the previous rulers. Josiah vowed to revive the covenant with God and keep all his commandments with all his soul and strength. Josiah stamped out all wickedness in the land and brought back the old practices and decrees in accordance with the piece of the Bible they found in the Temple. 2 Kings 23:25 sates that, "Neither before nor after Josiah was there a king like him who turned to the LORD as he did—with all his heart and with all his soul and with all his strength, in accordance with all the Law of Moses."

Josiah believed that he was ordained by God to return Israel to God when he found and read the Bible. In the same way, Eko finds the hatch and video inside and immediately knows they are important. Unlike Locke, Eko believes that pushing the button is now "more important than ever" and takes the notebooks in case they are useful in some way. Eko has put his whole trust into value of this new find, and consequently, the lives of the other survivors.

Trusting in God's plan is a critical part of our relationship with God. Jeremiah 29:11 says, "'For I know the plans I have for you,' declares the LORD, plans to prosper you and not to harm you, plans to give you hope and a future.'" God knows everything that will happen in your life and has a wonderful plan for it if you only let him direct your path as it states in Proverbs 16:9: "The mind of a man plans his way, but the LORD directs his steps." If you trust your life in his hand, it will be in good hands indeed, for God says, "Before I formed you in the womb I knew you, before you were born I set you apart; I appointed you as a prophet to the nations" (Jeremiah 1:4-5).

Do you trust God's plan for your life?

_____

_____

_____

_____

_____

_____

Are you willing to carry out anything God has in store for your future?

What is God's Plan? 145

"God made a better story. But it's a long story with a complicated plot & we're not very attentive readers."
–C.S. Lewis

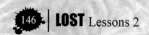

A Monumental Sacrifice

Episode 22
"Three Minutes"

In this episode's flashback, we learn what happened to Michael during his 13 days with the Others. He has made a deal with their leader "Mr. Friendly" and the matron base camp leader Ms. Klugh, to return to his camp, release Henry and betray Jack, Kate, Sawyer, and Hurley. If he does this, Michael and Walt will be set free and given a way off the island. Desperate to be reunited with his son at any cost, Michael willingly agrees to betray his friends. Once back at the survivors' camp, Michael starts to put the plan in motion, but Sayid is on to him. Sayid advises Jack that he strongly suspects Michael is a traitor. The episode ends during the funeral for Ana Lucia and Libby, when the survivors see a boat sailing near the beach.

In this episode and the last few we really see Michael doing whatever it takes to get what he wants. He is willing to commit murder and betray his friends to free Walt. This reminds us of the account of Judas in the Bible. Like Michael, Judas betrayed his friend to gain what he wanted most. In Luke 21:37- 22:47, we see Judas betraying Jesus so that He could gain riches and approval from the leaders of the church of that era. Judas was driven by deceit and greed that was powered by the devil himself (Luke 22:3).

Although faulted for betraying Jesus, Judas did fulfill what was predicted in the Old Testament and really had a part in one of the greatest things of all times, salvation. Jesus knew exactly what he was getting into when he came to earth. He knew he would have to suffer through tremendous beatings, physical and emotional turmoil, and a spiritual condition that He was not used to (his separation from God). But Jesus was committed to accomplishing His goals. He was willing to sacrifice himself for the sake of others.

In that same way, God was able to sacrifice His Son, Jesus, so that we all could be promised a better future. Through Jesus, God gave His everlasting love to a sinful world. He paid a big price to save the world through his son who was most dear to him. John 3:16 reminds us that, "For God so loved the world, that He gave His only begotten Son." Jesus came not only to bear our sins, but also to die for us as our sacrifice.

Although it is hard to see past Judas' betrayals and lies, God used these actions as a way to gain something much greater. Every person who believes in Jesus Christ for salvation is forever secure in Him.

We have been redeemed out of slavery forever. As Colossians 1:16 says, "For he (Jesus) has rescued us from the dominion of darkness and brought us into the kingdom of the Son he loves." And now because of the sacrifice, we have been saved.

But this is just the beginning of the story for a Christian. Our personal salvation story is part of a much larger epic story. Salvation is not the end all of what Christianity is about - it's just the beginning. Ephesians 2:8-10 says, "For it is by grace you have been saved, through faith—and this is not from yourselves, it is the gift of God— not by works, so that no one can boast. For we are God's handiwork, created in Christ Jesus to do good works, which God prepared in advance for us to do." We were created to be part of God's plan that he is working out throughout all time for the entire earth and heavenly realms to once again be under His perfect and ultimate control. He has created us with a job to do - we have a role to play a part in His Kingdom.

Our personal salvation enters us into God's Kingdom and God's plan to not only redeem us, but his plan for the redemption of all things in heaven and earth. The amazing thing is that we get to be a part of what God is doing throughout all of history. We get to be a part of how God is winning back His people.

As Ephesians 1:9-10 says, "He made known to us the mystery of his will according to his good pleasure, which he purposed in Christ, to be put into effect when the times reach their fulfillment—to bring unity to all things in heaven and on earth under Christ."

What is the main point of the betrayal, although it seems the most poignant?

_____

_____

_____

_____

_____

The Fulfillment of the Law comes shines the betrayal in what way?

_____

_____

_____

_____

_____

A Monumental Sacrifice

The Salvation of the people of this world could not have come without what? What did God have to sacrifice in order for us to come to Him?

_____

_____

_____

_____

_____

"They put on a front that appears accommodating, loyal, and yes, even sacrificial. Then, without warning, they raise their knife, and by the time you see the glint of the blade, it's almost always too late."

–Les Parrot

What Pushes your Button?

Episode 23/24
"Live Together, Die Alone"

The season two finally opens on Libby and Ana Lucia's funeral. As the funeral ends, a boat is spotted not far from the beach. Immediately Jack, Sayid, and Sawyer swim out to the boat only to find Desmond in the cabin drunk and disorientated. Locke, after previously trying to stop Mr. Eko in pushing the button, finds Desmond and takes the opportunity to get his help in running down the timer.

Meanwhile, Jack, Hurley, Kate and Sawyer are leaving with Michael to the other side of the island to find Walt and the others. As they travel, Kate realizes that the group is being followed and opens fire on their pursuers. The group kills one but the other escapes and the group, except Jack, wants to follow him. Jack reveals that he and Sayid knew that Michael has been lying to them the whole time and that he and Sayid have made a plan. Trying not to arouse suspicion of the others, the group pretends to still trust Michael and follow him to the other's camp. Sayid, who went to the Others camp by way of boat, lit a signal fire for the group which showed that Michael was actually taking them to some other place than the other's camp. As soon as they find this out though the group is shot with darts that makes them all fall to the ground, leaving them helpless for the others to capture.

John Locke earlier in the season is considered a man of faith. This faith that he had, was in his purpose on the island. He believed they were all there for a reason, and his duty on the island was to push the button in the hatch. However, his faith in the island was completely destroyed when they went to the other hatch and watched a video that Locke interpreted to mean that they were completing a trite task. The idea that the whole hatch was a farce did not just destroy his faith in the island, but destroyed his purpose for being on the island. He begins to believe that his whole existence was worthless, and it does not matter how he acts. Locke makes a big decision; he decides to let the timer run out without punching in the numbers.

Many people in our world today put their faith and purpose in things of this world. They base their lives in things like popularity, sports, and money; only to realize later that what they put their hope in has no meaning or substance. There is a very old Jewish story that occurs just after Abraham's calling in Genesis 12 that makes this point well. It was a story told by

Rabbis about the night that Abraham was getting ready to leave his father's household. They say that Abraham went into the large room of his father's house where all the statues of gods and idols were kept, and they say that Abraham went in and took an axe and broke everyone of the gods except for one. He then took the axe and placed it in the remaining statues hands. The next morning Abraham's father comes in and asks, "What has happened here?" To which Abraham replies, "I think it's quite clear what has happened here." To which Abraham's father replies, "No, it can't be. These are lifeless idols, I carved them myself out of brick, and stone, and marble, and wood. They are lifeless." To which Abraham replies, "Then why do you bow down to them"

    Another story that relates to this specific episode of Lost is Solomon. 1 Kings 11:4 says, "As Solomon grew old, his wives turned his heart after other gods, and his heart was not fully devoted to the Lord his God, as the heart of David his father had been." Solomon, like Locke, had been mislead and thought that life was meaningless. Because of this, Solomon thought that he was not a slave to anything and could do as he liked with no repercussions. Thankfully he later understood that his life belonged to God and returned to Him.

In this episode in we learn that John has devoted his life to this button, until suddenly he thinks it is a mere button and useless. John claims, "It's not real, none of it is real." John is forced to make a decision, is the button is useless, lifeless, and meaningless or it is of the utmost importance? The same can be said about Christianity. As C. S. Lewis states, "Christianity, if false, is of no importance, and if true, of infinite importance. The only thing it cannot be is moderately important."

What, in your life, do you have complete faith in?

_____

_____

_____

_____

_____

Can that faith be questioned, and give you doubt?

_____

_____

_____

How do you handle your faith in God being questioned?

___

___

___

___

___

___

Have you ever had an encounter with God that confirmed your believes? If so, how did it affect you?

___

___

___

___

___

___

___

___

"Christianity, if false, is of no importance, and if true, of infinite importance. The only thing it cannot be is moderately important." –C. S. Lewis

What Pushes your Button? | 159

"Faith is the art of holding on to things your reason has once accepted in spite of your changing moods"
–C. S. Lewis

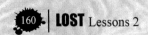

About the Authors

Dr. Randy T. Johnson has been married to Angela for over 25 years. They have two children, Clint and Stephanie. He has been Chaplain and Bible teacher at Oakland Christian School in Auburn Hills, Michigan for 20 years. He also ministers at two local Chinese Church youth groups. He wrote And Then Some, created Read316.com., and co-authored LOST Lessons.

David Rutledge has been working in youth ministry for over 10 years as a Bible teacher, a youth pastor and a speaker. David has a degree in Biblical Studies/Christian Education of Youth and History from Cedarville University, a Masters of Education from Regent University and is currently finishing up his Doctorate of Education from Liberty University. David lives with his wife Rebekah and children in Burbank California. He co-authored LOST Lessons.

Made in the USA
Lexington, KY
04 August 2011